T0005904

Advance Praise

Bruce Meyer is one of the most erudite, passionate poets writing today. The proof is this book of poems about poets, a tour de force which could only have been written by someone of Meyer's breadth of reading and depth of understanding. Each of these poems is a meditation on the nature of poetry and the madness of the poet's calling. Like the harmony of the spheres, these poems resonate with a music only the cosmos or a crazy poet can hear...
— *Max Layton, author of The Garden of I Am*

In an age of rampant materialism, it is wonderful to read the work of a poet who has kept the faith in otherwise seemingly ephemeral things— the breath we breathe in poetry and prayer, the quality we seek and find in the nature of a great question, reminding us of the soothing anodyne of memory and dream and of the powerful elixir of a fertile imagination. Meyer measures time by the millennial rhythms of the seasons as they occur over the span of lives long past and through their ever-present spirits. In his highly literate poetry we drink full from the cup of rain as it falls on the river and an inner thirst is quenched.
— *John B. Lee, Poet Laureate of Brantford and Norfolk County*

There is great virtuosity at work in this generous and elegant volume but Meyer never allows the technique to distract from his bright truths and wisdom. One gets the impression of a master poet at ease with his powers, intent on celebration, remembrance and clarity. Which is not to say that there aren't startling images and quotable lines in every poem. In fact the deceptively simple approach belies the rich mythic underlay which readers of his works both scholarly and poetic have come to expect. a book about poets but more than that a book about poetry itself. Or as Meyer says:

> *"This is not a chronicle of what is lost*
> *but celebration of what cannot be taken:"*
— *Robert Priest, author of The Mad Hand and Reading the Bible Backwards*

THE MADNESS
OF PLANETS

THE MADNESS
OF PLANETS

Bruce Meyer

Black Moss
Press
2015

Library and Archives Canada Cataloguing in Publication

Meyer, Bruce, 1957-, author
    The madness of planets / Bruce Meyer.

Poems.
ISBN 978-0-88753-556-7 (paperback)

I. Title.

PS8576.E93M33 2015   C811'.54   C2015-906908-4

Author photo: Mark Raynes Roberts
Cover design & layout: by Jay Rankin
Editing: Alicia Labbe
Cover image printed with permission from *Shutterstock*.

Published by Black Moss Press at 2450 Byng Road, Windsor,
Ontario, N8W 3E8. Canada. Black Moss books are distributed in
Canada and the U.S. by Fitzhenry & Whiteside. All orders should
be directed there.

Fitzhenry & Whiteside **Black Moss**
195 Allstate Parkway EST. 1969 **Press**
Markham, ON
L3R 4T8

Black Moss would like to acknowledge the generous financial
support from both the Canada Council for the Arts and the Ontario
Arts Council.

ONTARIO ARTS COUNCIL
CONSEIL DES ARTS DE L'ONTARIO
an Ontario government agency
un organisme du gouvernement de l'Ontario

Canada Council   Conseil des arts
for the Arts   du Canada

Contents

When I investigate and when I discover that the forces of the heavens and the planets are within ourselves, then truly I seem to be living among the gods.
— *Leon Batista Alberti*

And if imagination cannot run
  To heights like these, no wonder; no eye yet
  E'er braved a brilliance that outshone the sun.
— *Dante, Paradiso, X, 46-49*

The Thaw

for Jared Carter

There is a moment in every rural spring
when snow vanishes from last year's furrows
and small nothings come again from nothing.

The shout of an open barn door to bring
in air and chase the months of sorrows
sounds from that moment in every rural spring

when washing appears to kite on a string,
and each day leads to longer tomorrows,
and small nothings come again from nothing.

Flatland and hill farms repeat, and repeating,
are a prayer of dust only a concession knows
in that moment in every rural spring

when pane ice is off the brook, and a sleeping
century of sluices runs in fast brown flows
so that something comes again from nothing,

leaving time, and change, and every green thing
to keep count. Poetry is life, life to interpose
life and death living in every rural spring,
so everything may come again from nothing.

A Dead Language

for Bruce Hunter

*"...but on Sundays and holy days we take on this physical form
and tarry here to sing the praises of our Creator."*
— *The Voyage of St. Brendan*

On a hearth surrounded by stories,
in faces, memories, and times to come
the dead language offers its thanks.
It blesses the silence in which it sleeps.
It blesses you for continuing to speak.
It owns an echo no one hears.

Everyone has a dead language inside,
perhaps the one you are speaking now.
The tongue recalls ancient voyages,
reveals the porridge-thick slur
leading to an undiscovered land.

No one speaks a word when you arrive.
You must learn another way
to share the life in what you see,
and never having seen the like of it,
build new words from grains of sand.

A Convocation of Eagles

for Andrew Brooks

When we were young men
with sharp eyes and hungers
no commonplace could feed,
we lay in the quad and watched
as the sky tried to portend
the coming of great things.

I have disappointed myself.
Reaching and failing is the art
of cutting diamonds into dust.
I failed because I became
as good as anyone in my generation
but fell short of being better.

They took my life from me,
but not my words. I stare
through binoculars at stars
I never learned the names for
and they stare back at me
not wanting to know mine.

At convocation, the wool
pulled over our eyes, reality
set in like winter stretching
into long nights when life

demanded our attention and we
set aside our dreams and maps

for places life said *stay in*
rather than *go to*. But the sky
is still there, still waiting
to embrace our best thoughts,
the madness of planets
we tell our fortunes by.

Asking Questions

for Marty Gervais

Everywhere you look there are answers,
but there are never enough questions
to go around. Questions make us human –
they are the reason we exist, the reason why
we were born. Do you want to have sex? Yes.
Questions are beautiful. Questions are God.

Great minds have great questions for God.
What is real love? Are there answers
to things that trouble us? Perhaps, yes
or maybe no, but it never hurts to ask questions,
incessant questions. We want to know why
the sky is blue and to ask is only human;

and at the heart of every question, the human
heart will not let us rest. It is a reporter. God,
did you make the sea? Why is there pain? Why
can't we fly even though we try? The answers
are there, but let's rephrase the questions.
To report on life is noble because a simple why

may reveal the real story. The subject will say yes,
there is a Santa Claus, that we are human
because it means we can grow into our questions
and can learn to ask the right ones of God

as He gives us more than rainbows as answers
and we are startled as we learn that the why

of a starry night is the answer to another why,
and perhaps a story with the lead line "Yes,
God exists and has questions for our answers,"
and we will understand Him, love what is human
about the way He cares because He is God
and is a student of time struggling with questions.

Interrogation is our history, pages of questions
in an empty exam hall, a pen scratching out *why*
on a page over and over again because God
in His way is as tested as we are. He writes yes
to everything. That is His way, and our human
silences are punctuated by a mind that answers

all the questions on every page with *Yes! Yes!*
guessing when asked why; for to err is human,
but in the case of God it makes for great answers.

At the White Horse Tavern

in memory of Dylan Thomas

Somewhere at the bottom of a poem
a poet will find what he desires,

drinking life to the lees, sailing
on currents the way ancient seas

resemble handwriting as rough winds
and tides reel their lines ashore

and shatter them double on the rocks.
New York tonight is growing smaller,

its streets are shrinking into corridors
of tall hotels so the best ideas

can fit into a haiku or the Gents loo
almost coffin-sized and stinking of beer.

The taxis imagine they are songs,
and the paths they weave weep

to be the trajectory of stars that cross
until they collide on sidewalks

so astrologers can observe predestinations
and warn the beautiful words ahead.

The Beat

in memory of Nik Beat

The last time I saw Nik
we sat in a hot glass booth
while a summer night
drenched in beads of starlight
listened beneath the stillness
of invisible stars.

Max Layton sat in.
He was going to play his guitar with Nik.
Brandon Pitts was also there.
We all agreed to keep in touch.

We talked of poetry and why mortal love
tries to make the world go round,
spinning like the proverbial basketball
on the fingertip of globe-trotting minds.

And as I walked along Bloor Street,
drinking the aftermath
of an endless summer night,
I wanted to squeeze every living moment
from the fruit of unripened time,

knowing that what cannot live forever
spun above me disguised as beauty
as I wrestled to keep the truth of life
locked like a secret inside
my words while wondering
why heaven wouldn't share its plan.

Island of Fortuitous Discovery

in memory of Chelva Kananganayakam

You were from that island
named for fortuitous discovery,
but it was I, a lost navigator,
who was fortunate to find you.

To ballads of strife and homeland tears
an island of pain and beauty
lay dying among the palms
in the brilliant green of stories

told on a south wind through fronds
wafted in your melodious voice;
and if I praised you for this now
you would blush shyly.

Kindness is what survives us,
and after having crossed the world
to share the legends of a place,
I name that place for you.

Counting Spider Plants

for James Deahl

You can write any damned poem you want.
    — *Michael Wurster*

When Milton Acorn opened his mouth to laugh,
I thought I saw the ruins of Dresden,
the delicate blackened antique walls
and sad porcelain figurines
broken yet smiling still
in the fire storm of his words.
His roar rattled the windows,
and our fists beat the air
for no other ever raised a monument to poetry
to compete with a gale-force shout.

And my great forgotten chroniclers of uncertainty
who passed through portals of rare words –
Marty Singleton as good as forgotten
but still as good,
and Brooks, and O'Riordan, and someone named Lawrence,
and James Deahl strung out on an air guitar
to summon angel tidings of great joy –

we sat in the web of spider plants
festooned around steamed grey windows
running tears where the rococo of pipe tobacco

struggled through proletarian Sundays
and made the air blue with azure beauty
in the lost diction of Snow Goose bardery.

For young men in the vagaries of words
are richer in undiscovered truths than kings
whose treasure waits in ambiguous silence
locked in rancid second-hand books
we passed from hand to hand as promises
on nights we held but could not keep
when we stumbled almost home to home,
knowing the spider would return to dine
to suck the blood from life's long sentence.

Halfway Across the Bridge

for John Berryman

Say what you say, a swim is
good anytime you feel too close
to yourself and Henry's phone,
I say Henry, answer your damned
phone, has been busy all day.
Sometimes you get so lonely
you forget how to talk to yourself,
assuming, of course, you remain
an intelligent, fine, up-standing
conversationalist. Don't make me
laugh. I'm laughing in the face
of death and he's got no goddamned
sense of humour until you stop
listening and that's when you know,
or should know, and can't know,
that he's split his guts at you,
while down there a barge-hand
smokes a cigarette and blows a blue
cloud toward me, and I know he's
having fun, he's going somewhere.
Yep. Gotta tell Henry that rivets
look like moles on a whore's back.

A Poem Against Metaphors

in memory of Tomas Transtromer

So don't breathe. Don't think
of a metaphor for breathing,

and don't pretend to hear
echoes of old poems bouncing

off the walls as one hears
silence transforming itself

into something so simple
it cannot help but be mistaken

for the real, heartfelt sobbing
of the man in the next apartment

who punctuates silences between
each sob with a cough or a train

clacking over suburban tracks
with one lonely woman sitting

in the light of an empty carriage
as she turns and looks up at you,

because, for an instant, you connect
and you are not anything else

than the one she holds in her mind.
Someday you will get together –

you, the man with the cough,
the woman in the train window,

and the train's engineer – and that
persistent cough that won't go away

even though it is almost summer,
and you'll recall the good time

you spent in a coincidence
when you were more than strangers,

almost friends, in who shared a night,
wish each other well, and promise

to spend milliseconds together again,
and you will weep and laugh,

then go your separate ways
as footsteps *soto voce* in the night.

Brown Shoes

for John B. Lee

A man wears brown shoes cautiously
because he doesn't know any better,
because in them he has seized the moment
when the chance for shoes presents itself
as he doesn't care if they match navy
or the shades of blackish grey in suits.

He wears brown shoes defiantly
because he has a fear of undertakers,
fears their dour, hushed-up voices,
does not want his wife to be afraid
of winter Sundays all by herself
or the sound of his chair sitting empty.

And wearing brown shoes too long
a man believes his moment has come
and dons white shoes for leisure
until the truth of his mortality sinks in
and he remembers his lost grandfather
for whom brown meant a life of work.

A man in comfortable brown shoes
knows they are the colour of earth,
knows a nostalgia for touching the soil
and remembers the strength Antaeus had

when Hercules held his coil aloft
and the giant shrank in the strong arms.

To touch the earth is no laughing matter:
the touch of earth is the need to feel,
a love of springtime, the clutch of mud,
the long held belief that earth feeds life,
and that no one dies pure of heart
unless he absolves the God of seasons.

A man wears brown shoes with hope
unafraid of mortal simplicities,
understands how time will grip him,
until the dust and the man are one
and the place he stands and his shoes
are of that element that longs for more.

Garden Party Artist

for Claire Weissman Wilks

Listen to the colour of azaleas,
a fountain conversing by a patio,

musicians playing in green shade,
and sunlight on white lawn chairs;

though time worked hard today,
laughter in the garden was stronger;

fine conversation, cool white wine,
exquisite food, friends, your home –

all in a generosity of spirit
that illustrates the joy of living,

the grace of here and now present
whenever happiness is framed,

in the figure of the heart's true art:
the good we share lasts forever.

Purity

for Laurence Hutchman and Eva Kolacz

The day admires itself
in the eyes of lovers,
promises blue skies
will be clear forever,
animates royal lilacs,
carpets of forget-me-nots
to voice a wedding day.

Spring is one excuse
for making promises,
but as good as any
because prayers rise
like songbirds on days
when the sky is new
and a mother robin
hovers over hatchlings.

The word today is desire,
not merely hunger,
but the hunger to feed
others that rich desire,
to share happiness
as heaven shares light:
for purity is what comes
of blue robin's eggs
hatched to the lilt of yes.

The Taste of Water

for Anna Yin

Sunshine plays on ripples of sound
as music carries the taste of water;

for what is pure says the *guzheng*
is a forest brook on a summer morning,

its melody flowing over moss and stones
to become nothing so beautiful as nothing,

the way a thought slips through a spider web
leaving only silver drops as reminders

that what sustains life the moment after
life is lived so it may live again

is what quenches the thirst for words;
a light to wet the lips with silence.

Li Po Walks in Greenwich Village and Remembers His Lover the Moon

So the sidewalk has luminosity
tonight because it intones yellow

from the street lamps and blues
from a sky that confesses its love

to the moon when she hides her face
and cries for the man in the coffee shop

whose words wounded her when she spoke
of love and eternal hope for beauty –

and why I look in storefront windows
on rainy nights such as this and watch

sad coats pleading to swing their sleeves
and hold each other's empty hands,

guarding the abandoned outpost of the moon
and the chance to die in each other's arms.

Tu Fu: The Journey Home

for David Wevill

> *Parted by death, we swallow remorse*
> *Apart in life, we always suffer.*
> — *"Dreaming of Li Po"*

1)

This morning in the first grey light
I heard voices from a nearby hut;
raising myself weakly on one elbow
saw an old woman and a boy arguing
over a dying rooster. One by the legs,
the other by the neck, they stretched the world
from it, offering the bird up to me at noon
as the sky darkened. The boatmen came.
They brought news of illness from father up,
messages of discontent, the fields on fire.
My mind was troubled. The heart felt nothing.
In all the long nights, with lovers or alone,
I believed in order – or was it peace? Seasons
slipped through my hand, always the blossoming
gave way, always an old friend parted
at the forking road. The dreams know more
as I grow older. Their cities are peopled
with faces I knew, the names downriver
awaiting my return. I grow weary, not

anxious, the journey, perhaps half a breath
into its next sentence, leaves me with
so much to say, so little permitted to say,
and my head on a pillow made of fallen wings.
The rain begins slowly like a prayer,
drawing to its meaning the moon and stars,
waves lapping as the night threads on,
the world outside forever wanting in.
The mind is too little to embrace it all.

2)

The cranes woke me. I thought they were
soldiers, their shadows just emerging
among the reeds, their long black necks bending
like willows along the bank as wind
moved them. The spirit of the summer
is everywhere but here. When a woman
startled them the birds took flight, rising,
pulling behind them with piercing shouts
the brightness of the morning sun high
above the buzzing village flies. The girl
who cooked my dinner was fifteen. That night
she came to sit beside me, holding my hand
as the sun turned red among the hillsides,
her eyes smooth and white as moons.
I touched her breast and she undid her tunic,
baring her small brown nipples for my kiss.
I remembered my first lover's face,

the smell of her belly brought back the earth,
the soil of my garden alive with flowers.
Her hair fell freely as she freed my shoulders,
her face against my face as if fire upon fire,
the fisherman's lamp of so many nights of travel,
the warmth of a brazier beside our mat,
the shape of her ribs like the farmlands and hills –
had I been a day younger her moans would have pleased me,
the river within her calmed and straight,
my boat well-built, its prow to the morning.
The sky was blackened when the cranes took flight.

3)

Do you know this river? It has always flowed,
perhaps not near you, but always with you,
its beat more constant than the words a poet
could give to all the things he loves. The reeds
are reflected when the water is still. I know
your eyes though we may not have met. They scan
the horizon for the presence of knowledge, for what
may be learned or simply recalled, the smell
by a riverbank when the rain has stopped,
the desire of bodies to be close in the night.
I knew your eyes would enter here, this boat
on a river, forgotten by hours, my voice
an echo given chance after chance, the wind
through the wind chimes repeating yet different,
moving by accident, struck with their purpose.

I received a letter from my friend, Yen Wu,
and this is my answer; I return through my wishes.
I wish on the waves that are constant as drums,
on the wind and the reeds and fields and their bones,
to be with you forever, to drink and laugh
and sit in your garden as the blossoms fall.
I think of my home and the river that leads there.
It flows within me, my wish to you.

Lives of the Poets

for Kerry Johnston

Every poet claims a piece of the world.
I have heard others sing of fathers,
of roads where seventh sons and magic
outstrip the failures of what we are
and give hope for what we want to be.
I have heard the lines where oceans
became the words of drowning men
as sunlight slipped a coin into their hands
before they learned to hold on to life.
And if every poet claims a world in words,
I want to claim the tapestry of your hands,
the stories they weave when what you say
becomes the trees moving to the wind,
the updraft in leaves before the rain,
the sound of rain as it falls in summer,
touching everything as if it feels,
to make what is green greener with its love,
each leaf a palm held out in thirst
to drink the poetry that is gone too soon,
yet quenches what the moment longed for.
I want to speak of the silence of your smile
when you know the world is made of days
and happiness as rare as sunlight on lake;
for in every story that you tell,
every legend of how we lived,

I want live among the heroes in the stars
when you lie beside me and you are dreaming
the poetry of a life you speak inside.

A Free Translation

in memory of Mavis Gallant

Language needed to be rebuilt with the cities
in the years after the war. Streets of crafted rubble

became attractive places where language rose
from ashes and pretended to be a phoenix.

Some remained untouched, and a good cup
of coffee and sunlight of a quieter era defined

the last gawking angels hanging from cornices
and mirrors trying to mend their own reflections

though the injury was not their fault. One by one.
great sentences could be reclaimed from memory,

and the few guidebooks left behind in fine hotels
contained enough clues to articulate lost beauty.

One day, while walking beside the city's river,
a golden bird lit on an old elm and told her a story.

Litany of the Makers

Now all my teachers are dead except silence
— W.S. Merwin, "A Scale in May"

1) Earle Birney: Endurance

Clutching all six feet and then some
of Earle under his arms and dragging
him from his bed to the stone window sill
so he could look down University Avenue
to catch a glimpse of his publisher's office,

I told him what he could not remember –
he was a poet with an obligation to words.
After hauling him back to his hospital bed
and settling the covers around him like a book,
I left a pad of paper and a ballpoint pen.

He told me he still dreamed in poems.
His old friend, my professor, Miller McClure,
had died in the next bed a week before,
reciting Milton as he fought death's angel.
Earle knew my name when I arrived.

As last autumn light flooded Earle's room
and time drowned him in seas of imagination,
he penned his final poems. We had stood
on his balcony years before, floating city-wise,
to discuss the battle of time against voice.

39

Some things are left undone and others
better left unsaid, though I cannot think
of a journey I would rather embark upon
than one into the wilderness with Earle
if only there is ink and paper there to write on.

A poet's reputation is almost a butterfly –
from pupa to chrysalis, cocoon to wings.

The journey is long and the wind against him.
He must find a home among the fallen trees

and feed on flowers that bloom without him.
Ray was wrapped in white sheets, his eyes

so keen like Milton he had lost his vision,
or Tiresias, a Sibyl in a basket knowing more

than my head could contain. He memorized
my poems, recited works by others as well,

pointed to book stacks he had learned by heart
that went to the bottomless sea of his memory.

Take something with you, he requested. Release
them to the world. The art of being a poet is flight –

not yours, not your ego or even your soul –
but words – words that rise startled at the sound

of daylight on an autumn morning when you
know there is only one direction home and passion

seen in the face of life shrivelling within sends
them home, each wing a beating heart, defying gravity.

3) Irving Layton: Passion

Where in the passion of poetry
comes a miraculous light?
I saw the scant oil in the temple.
Days I watched it burn bright.

I should have made a pilgrimage
to hold the old man's hand,
but there would be no verse in it,
just a vision of an uncertain land...

always fight in his eyes;
angry storms, thunder shouts
against the Philistine brick wall.
His fists battered by endless bouts

where he took punches, snarled,
ranted until his light dwindled,
lion mane aged to gentle snow.
The fire spoke what Yahweh kindled.

O! The tabernacle of mortal desire!
But even that ran its course.
His gaze cleared to staring eyes,
his voice gentled, he grew hoarse,

and gradually said no more.
In this country of such feeble voices
snows bury everything in silence
and conjure more youthful Messiahs.

I have seen the passion of poetry,
a miraculous light, a dwarf spark,
passed by word among our few,
a dream of shadows in the dark.

4) Dorothy Livesay: Language

When you put the tip of your words
on the consonant end of my tongue

I thought of the lost beauty of the world
and how I would have kissed you
had you still been young.

The pity of the phrases we pronounce
is that, like mirrors of our souls,

they outlive us as we denounce
what time takes from you, unredeemed,
and we peer through worm holes

of an old book and try to read it differently.
Across time itself, our imprimatur

inked in black blood for all to see
leaves a shadow impression on the page
and is neither time's disease nor time's cure.

Leading the life of an island when ships pass by
I walked alone tonight in the afterglow
and imagined shores without a single footprint,

the inner labyrinth of green life a lexicon,
and every clear stream a perfect memory.
I called to you in the twilight once –

the shadows buzzed with cicadas.
You held a white flower in your fingertips,
its petals draping your articulate hand,

waiting to be pressed like a poem among pages,
set to memory as if a round summer moon.
Season after season I clutch the brittle remains

of the old earth's crumbling catalogue,
tighten my knuckles to white and nothing I can say
can restore the light to a withered rose

or the moon high in a humid August sky
unless someone in the silence of a winter night
needs and is needed to announce the first star.

Starlight, star bright, I knew a woman who sang
of the plucked moon blooming on an August night.
She gave me the white flower in her hand.

6) Al Purdy: Voice

The day had been made in Hades
the way history is thwarted by time
and there's never enough Canadian beer
to wash the air's passion clean
as a starlit November night.
Through the kitchen window
the lost mill of the Roblins
left its reflection in the lake
and a dying seagull
a relic from an old Coleridge number
flopped on the front lawn
as thirsty as a pilgrim of life
but too exhausted to drink anymore.
Halfway through a leak off your porch
you turned to me and noted
with the efficiency of a scholar in your voice
that you'd tried to write your name with water
but wished it had been one syllable less for penmanship
or you'd had just one beer more for pressure.
And I recalled this is the way the animals
mark the boundaries of their minds
their names carved in the scent they leave
with a glass of everything they have taken in
saying simply this is my place
and I will live in it or die.
There is never enough to fill us
though we pour for others
and our names are written on water

not by it
and the ink lake
close enough to see but just far enough so as not to be
touched
caught the image of a passing cloud
that looked for all the world like an old plough
and fed it to the mill as grist.
Here my spreading Protean friend
is a promise I made to you as that dying albatross
hungered for the sky even as it clutched the ground
that wherever I sail
whatever zephyrs press me on
I shall write my name on a wall or passing rock
to declare the truth that I was here
measuring my thoughts in syllables and piss
that a common man might take for history
the way you taught me
when we gave our names to the earth.

In those few untimed moments
between a dawn's red sky
and emergence of the sun,

first bars of a daylight sonata
begin in the winter silence.
Life is always another recital.

If one plays from the soul
the score becomes a world,
the dusted hills and *arpeggios*

defiant, elegant clef leaves
falling gently on North Hatley –
the rest, the *continuo* of wind,

a heart's cadenza *pianissimo*,
as hands leave the keys
and the next note – that voice

so close to beauty – is mute...
and it is plausible though not probable
the act of listening is love,

a devotion to resolution
for an instant, then relinquished,
a gift to the north wind.

Light was a scripture
pouring through the mission's windows
as she wrestled with a God
who had taken everything from her
save only the love of God shared with her as manna.

He had taken her life
her poetry
her picnics and the history
that once dwelt in her veins.
He had taken the summers
leaving her only that beauty
that reviles the stupidities and vanities,
sparrow twitters twisting the streets,
common culture clattering over which God casts
an indifferent eye,
a blind, blind eye.

Her mother was dying eternally.
        The world was contained in a mustard seed.
Lilies blossomed in a field somewhere.
Poetry wanted her to smell them.

But poetry is only God's art if God writes it.
It is a gift that comes as if a flood tide
on a winter morning,
evidence of things hoped for,
realities of the unimaginable,

a present tied to the end of a string
tethering a flight of angels.

And standing on the edge of a cold ocean
she could not dip her foot in it
            but saw far off the whiteness in the divine gaze,
endless horizon returning stare for stare.
God loves her.

God made her promise that every word
was His and His alone to use
the word made into spring
            so far out of reach that death bragged
in his shade that he had won
that he had shut out the light from her mission
and after all was said and done
He had bigger words to deal with –
the one sitting on the vast abyss
to impregnate our open mouths...

and waiting for it, hungry, a street person
shivering in the cold
she knew his belly could not eat
what his mind and heart could not fathom
and only the love of God
could move the beggar to ask for more.

9) John Newlove: Image

i)

The plovers circle
over grass lands
and wind waves
wash at horizons.

Hearing the hooves
riding against sky
black figures pursuing
the buffalo herds

death prefigured history
as history itself
became a prophecy
down among saskatoons

in shaded coulees.
The past inebriates
drunkards the soul
tells clever lies

to the prairie
gives bones aches
and wind waves
wash at horizons.

ii)

The last time
I saw him
his panama hat
and cream suit

were disappearing down
Ottawa's Wellington Street
the paper perfume
hanging on fingers

day after day
debating official languages.
The medicine wheel
atop Blue Hills

aligned to constellations
was an eye
seeing beyond horizons
where the world

not only ends
but begins again
the bleached forevers
of hoof beats.

The riders come
seeking an end

and it is
only a beginning.

iii)

Three riders came
three black clouds
after a tornado
narrowly passed Wilcox

leaving a swath
cut into legumes
the steady wheat
nodding at clouds.

Tell the sunsets
they are clocks.
Tell time life
is not mastered

by passing seasons.
Riders will come
seeking the place
where winds wait

and plovers circle
over the grass
as the eye
reads all horizons.

Nature lives in what dies to live again.
There are days when I struggle to find
a word for tangled undergrowth,
that bramble from which faces emerge
to worship at the shrine of mystery.
You had grown a new tooth.
The locals went out at night,
transformed into harp seals,
and mated on the rocks of Falmouth harbour.
The gulls strove toward a winter sun.
The world remains a miracle of entropy,
and looking up we saw a shooting star,
the shared destiny of a moment's realization.
A green man stepped from the copse
hard by St. Biddulph's abandoned shrine.

Hard by St. Biddulph's abandoned shrine
a green man stepped from the copse,
the shared destiny of a moment's realization,
and looking up we saw a shooting star.
The world remains a miracle of entropy.
The gulls strove toward a winter sun
and mated on the rocks of Falmouth harbour.
Transformed into harp seals,
the locals went out at night.
You had grown a new tooth
to worship at the shrine of mystery,
that bramble from which faces emerge,

a word for tangled undergrowth.
There are days when I struggle to find
nature lives in what dies to live again.

11) Visiting P.K : Patience

There is a woman floating in a window –
transparent –
Christmas wreaths in passing houses
shine now in eye and now in hair, in heart.
        — "Reflection in a Train Window"

There is a woman floating in a window,
and light through Venetian blinds
transforms her into bars of music,
mystical and almost transparent.
Do you like Philip Glass, she asks?
Victoria buried by a sudden snow,
her garden city is a Christmas world.
The kettle boiled, she wets the tea
and through steam and filigree shadow
there is a woman floating in a window.

Transparent –
that is the word I want to give to her,
the way light makes poetry of her face,
the eyes that remind me of an icon,
hair that reflects the soft voice of angelic
nuances hidden in language crafted with an accent
that echoes to the dithyrambic turnings
of Glass music filling the house
like wind chimes making the dissonant
transparent –

Christmas wreaths in passing houses
my cab passed on the way here this day
are life buoys in a sea of sudden snows
and not entirely out of place among
her thoughts on poetry: we talk of *Preview*,
Patrick Anderson, Judith Cape, the muses
of Modern verse, and where retired
inspirations go as if a poet ever said no
to what she could hold on to; seasons, causes,
Christmas wreaths in passing houses...

Shine now in eye and now in hair, in heart
that memory should set you in the window there,
a winter sun making you even more serene,
more of what I remember now – the snow –
flecking your steel grey hair, shining
trees bent beneath their weight, the subtle start
to a new year, perhaps another poem.
Thank God memory is an ageless place
like the inside of a glosa. Let the art
shine now in eye and now in hair, in heart.

A cold cutting stone chipped in igneous
and foreign to the island's sandstone –
turning it over in your hand you told us
it contained a woman's face – cheekbone

carved for grip and stripping
meat from a blood-warm kill,
the nose aquiline, mouth drooping,
the sadness, the eyes dark and still

staring on and on into a gorged sea.
The fog pronounced each breathing thing
in its own smooth voice: myth, destiny,
a pile of bones. Did she sing

of a sadness that brought her strength?
Or was the stone her alibi, aboriginal,
abnormal, waiting for the arms-length
of time to take her to those abysmal

islands called memory, recollection,
the living past? Tell me again the one
about the hunger, wind in transgression
against the world's flesh, the aching bone

split open by its own marrow, the rocks
sharing no secrets except their soft red
fury cut from the cracked sea backs
of legends? I can't believe you are dead.

An elder, an ancestor carved her grief.
The granite lives to pay the cost
and like granite you offered up relief.
One good story or we are lost.

13) Eli Mandel: Process

Opened onto Prairie
where his ancestors lay

the door into nowhere
began in his garden

buried in the wilderness
of time and ancient faith.

At family gatherings
sacred words are read

and the scent of spirits
from the open bar

reminds me we believe
in a life everlasting

we cannot pronounce
when actual life departs.

If you set foot in nowhere,
if you meet yourself

on a summer's day,
remember eternal life

is beyond mortal reach
except for the phrases

we send as delegates
to look back on us with love.

14) Philip Larkin: Moment

Monuments in an age of missed opportunities –
how a need for long matches to light a cooker
should intervene on the course of poetries;
how a woman and an ill-spoken shopkeeper

should hold me long enough at a tobacconist's
to miss meeting you. That is broken rhyme.
Perhaps you were the bespectacled illusionist
disappearing down Piccadilly? Another time.

Every missed opportunity dwells in sadness
the way rain on a London sidewalk is a mirror
for magistrates or arbiters of taste, madness
and anything else of value in a daft culture

that is a marvel of incomplete design. A bridge
remains unfinished. A crane appears to shrug
atop an office tower, on blank pages, that edge
of then and now. The sky numbs us like a drug.

15) Bronwen Wallace: Memory

The surgeon excised
part of my lips
but none of my memory
in an act of prevention
and winter surgery
where I saw my words
torn away from me
and in a Tylenol dream
and north wind pain
of lost words spoken
that hover before us
you came to me
to bless me with
the beauty of speech.
Your mouth bandaged
your eyes spoke pages
pouring through streets
of a Kingston paved
in granite and unredeemed
oceans of lost creatures.
Our narratives met
at a street corner
where we turned
and went the same way
in a purple winter light
upon us with grace
a simplicity in language
liberating the sidewalks

with news we
are not measured by
what kills us but by
what we choose to live by –
threads of testimony
left as snowy footprints
attesting to the equality
of hearts tempered
by stones we instruct
in the parables of feeling –
we leave behind us
the gift of narratives
or the shadows we cast
beneath yellow street lamps
the remnants of the human
the being who never dies
because his or her stories
refuse to die and out live
their telling because they
are the things that lived
not just beyond us
or outside the grasp
of the way we record love
but in others
long after the daylight
has turned to mythology
and we must find
something to believe in.

16) James Reaney: Identity

On the dusty road from Lucan I had a vision
of a demi-Eden where a man might simply hold
in the palm of his hand like a toy block
the entire world, and for a moment I thought
the sky had become a theatre and all play
was an obligation for a king who loved magic.

The play's the thing. A county of rough magic
could transform a blasted oak or mere vision
of a barn into a cosmos, and trees at play
in summer wind were dancers reaching to hold
the sun in the sky long after an afterthought
became a landmark or simply another roadblock.

Here was a county thirsting for rain, a block
of concessions laid in chains where magic
and mortal fascination (plot, character, thought,
diction, spectacle, and song) were an almanac vision
foretelling those simple human truths that hold
the mind and soul in awe or tear a heart at play.

I am being dramatic because to see a play
about ourselves is like a mirror that can block
the shadow of age and make us remember the hold
love once had on us or the abject terror of magic
and mystery that haunted childhood, the vision
we had for life in things and worlds in a thought.

And when his birds spoke Chaucerian love I thought
this is part of the great conversation, the interplay
of ideas across time, the obligation to poetic vision
one must pass by word or word of mouth to block
the thanatic, memory without remembrance, for magic
works constantly to transform what it cannot hold.

And so my obligation is to set things free, a hold
like Excalibur's to be cast away, the begotten thought
that is now yours because you share this rough magic.
And if I take my book and drown it, the play
of wind on a brown field, a chip off the old block,
will wash it back on you and script your vision.

The longer we hold this faith, the more the play
will draw every thought from us and block
our fear of magic and transform our merest vision.

17) Northrop Frye, Seated

If there was snow in his hair yesterday
it is gone now. The sun has illumined
the gold that was once a scholar's cap.
Bronze belongs in murmurs the way
time belongs in a clock; but in the dimmed
world of ideas things change. I stop

to remember him, enshrined like a line
of prose caught in a footnote, referencing
something greater than itself, a heartbeat
that refused its down-stroke, the fine
iamb given an incomplete grade, a surfacing
in greenish skin. They caught you being great.

If I am remembered it will be the way chalk
is remembered in the sills and crevices
of rooms where ideas were spent like dimes
in junked payphones, yattered small talk
about the weather of an obvious day that ices
over and melts, promising warmer times.

I have not forgotten how your hand
shook mine, how the clasp of lineage
was a conversation going back to Chaucer,
how you taught me that ideas stand
time better than monuments, and age
gracefully as shadows from year to year.

And in your hand, a hand once warm
from dancing on thoughts and keys,
you hold a book of secrets someone made
and you read it as a sailor reads a storm,
smiling confidently. The horizon says
voyage forth with a map of dream in my head.

18) Elegy for Jack Gilbert

Maybe it is more than just what remains.
What continues to remain. What outlasts.
Not the absence but the challenge to the void.
Not the silence but the voice in silence.
No one is able to speak for the dead.
Only the living are conversant in life.
The dead articulate their muted tongue.
The living must retreat to themes:
love, longing, grief lessoned in memory.
Such are the means to speak of the moment.
Elegies struggle with a lifetime's pain.
A way to argue that life is stronger.
Stronger for the living. A hunger for tomorrow.
Walk by the sea on a low tide morning.
Each grain of sand was once a lifespan.
A bleached welk tangles the tide weed,
an outer bone that survived the world.
Not the creature that lived in the shell,
but the shell itself, the iridescent interior.
The inside shining. The spiralled mystery.
Sunlight that enters the coral chamber.
The sound of an ocean alive inside.
The living need to hear it survives.
Need to learn of ways to speak for life.
Words from the buried heart in the chamber.
The storm passes the way dreams pass.
Jetsam strewn haphazard on shores.
The shell is proof of the life it is has been.

70

The story that repeats the sea.
The record that outlasts the depths.
The narrative that refuses to die.
This is not a chronicle of what is lost
but celebration of what cannot be taken:
the enumeration of life's sure strength.

19) Seamus Heaney: Dawn

i.m. August 30, 2013

Yellow hedgerow gorse blinked and fell
at summer's end on a hill slope waking wet
in dewy blessing. Sun sang in each bauble.
Fields clasped rosaries of ancient starlight.

It is time, sky and humbled clouds rolled on,
for silence to learn the silence of fierce sleep,
to learn the world's living voice alive again
risen from pain to life to love to live in the deep

earthen footprints of fattened flocks grazing
the worried slides. Words are carved on wind
and filter boughs of father oaks phrasing
a spell from what was said and left behind,

never to be forgotten the way a shadow shows
the outline of a body wherever the soul goes.

20) Benediction

To love language as much as life
is to fly in the face of time and death,
to see reality edited with a knife,
to know a life's work is not enough
to love language as much as life.
The art of speaking to silence is tough
but the memory of sound and breath
is a love of language as much as life
that flies in the face of time and death.

And knowing them set my life afloat.
Remembering them, I dream them back,
for aside from books or an occasional note,
they have left only patterns they wrote;
yet knowing them set my life afloat.
Poems are consequential: they are about
a shout on paper left silent and black:
yet knowing them has kept my life afloat.
Reciting by heart, I dream them back.

The poet, critic, lunatic, and lover
are the errant knights of a neglected art;
yet I remember them as if they hover
before me on a battlement to recover
for the poet, critic, lunatic, and lover
what death took from life but not the soul. Other
voices will take up their words – the part

of the poet, critic, lunatic, and lover –
to embrace the spell of a neglected art.

Acknowledgements

"Tu Fu: The Journey Home," appeared previously in *The Open Room* (Black Moss Press, 1989). "A Free Translation" appeared in *Exile Literary Quarterly*, and was shortlisted for the 2014 Gwendolyn MacEwen Prize for Poetry. "Raymond Souster: Vision," appeared in a tribute anthology for Raymond Souster edited by James Deahl. *A Litany of of the Makers* appeared as a limited edition chapbook, (Lyrical Myrical Press, 2014). "Gwendolyn MacEwen: Advocacy," appeared previously as "The White Flower" in *The Open Room* (Black Moss Press, 1989). "Visiting P.K.: Patience" appeared previously as "Visiting P.K." in the anthology of *Glosa's for P.K. Page* edited by Jesse Patrick Ferguson and published by Buschek Books; and in *A Book of Bread* (Exile Editions, 2012). "Seamus Heaney: Dawn" and "Brown Shoes" appeared in *Testing the Elements* (Exile Editions, 2014). Many thanks to Professor Juan de Dios Cabellero Torallbo, Luciano Iacobelli, Michael Callaghan, David Wevill, Halli Villegas, David Bigham, James Deahl, Jared Carter, John B. Lee, Bruce Hunter, Laurence Hutchman, Jason Rankin, Alicia Labbe, Karen Wetmore and the staff of Grenville Printing at Georgian College for their generosity of thought and their useful feedback. And, as always, a very special thank you to Kerry, Katie, Margaret, and Dr. Carolyn Meyer, the muses of my world. Thank you Marty Gervais for your continued belief in my work.

About the Author

Bruce Meyer is author of forty six books of poetry, short fiction, non-fiction, literary journalism, and textbooks. His most recent works include the short story collection, *A Chronicle of Magpies*, the poetry collections *Testing the Elements*, *The Arrow of Time* and *The Seasons* (a book of one hundred love sonnets in the tradition of Pablo Neruda that garnered Meyer the silver IP Medal from the Independent Publishers' Association of America and runner-up status for the Indie Fab Foreword Prize for the best book of poems published in North America in 2014). His work has been shortlisted for the Montreal International Poetry Prize and the Exile-Vanderbilt Short Fiction Prize. His broadcasts with Michael Enright on *The Great Books* (3 volumes), *A Novel Idea*, and *Great Poetry: Poetry is Life and Vice Versa*, remain the CBC's bestselling spoken word series. With Black Moss Press he has recently published the very popular *Dog Days: A Comedy of Terriers* (poetry), *Time of the Last Goal: Why Hockey Is Our Game* (poetry, fiction, and non-fiction), the novel in poetry *The Obsession Book of Timbuktu*, and co-edited *The White Collar Book* (an anthology of white collar work) with Carolyn Meyer. He lives in Barrie, Ontario where he was the inaugural Poet Laureate for the City. He is professor of Creative Writing and Communications at Georgian College, and Visiting Professor of Comparative Literature at Victoria College in the University of Toronto.